J 796.332 HETRICK
Hetrick, Hans,
Football's Record Breakers /
33341007990467

P9-CJZ-908

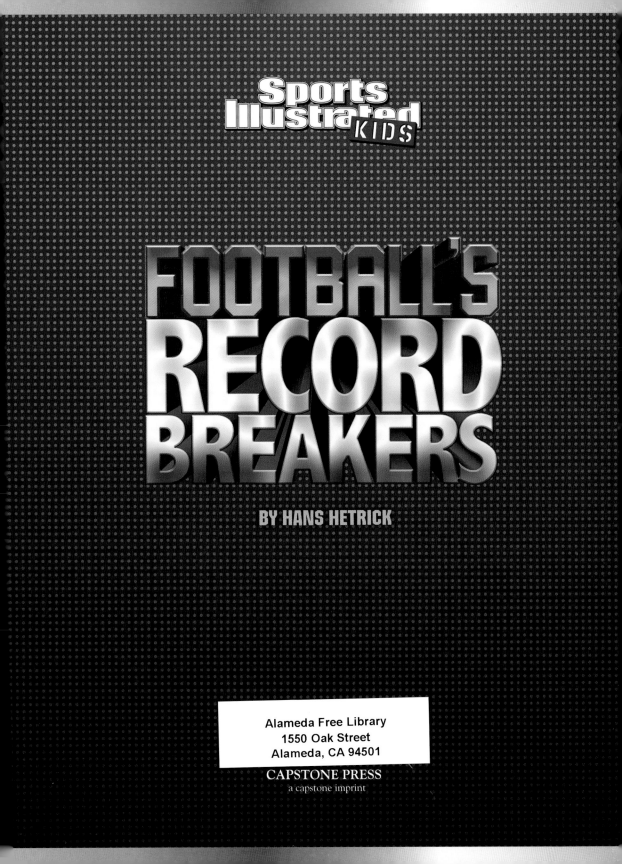

Sports Illustrated KIDS

FOOTBALL'S RECORD BREAKERS

BY HANS HETRICK

CAPSTONE PRESS
a capstone imprint

Sports Illustrated Kids Record Breakers is published in 2017
by Capstone Press, 1710 Roe Crest Drive, North Mankato, Minnesota 56003
www.mycapstone.com

Library of Congress Cataloging-in-Publication Data is available on the Library of Congress website.

Sports Illustrated Kids is a trademark of Time Inc. Used with permission.

ISBN 978-1-5157-3761-2 (library binding)
ISBN 978-1-5157-3765-0 (paperback)
ISBN 978-1-5157-3774-2 (eBook PDF)

Editorial Credits
Nick Healy, editor; Veronica Scott, designer; Eric Gohl, media researcher;
Gene Bentdahl, production specialist

Photo Credits
AP Photo: Beth A. Keiser, 29, Peter Read Miller, 10, Vernon J. Biever, 16; Getty Images: Bettmann, 22, Focus On Sport, 18, 26 (top), John Biever, 14, 15, Mickey Pfleger, 4, Vincent Muzik, 28; Newscom: UPI Photo Service/Billy Suratt, 27 (top); Shutterstock: EKS, cover; Sports Illustrated: Andy Hayt, 26 (bottom), Bill Frakes, 12, Heinz Kluetmeier, 13, 20, John Biever, 11, 19, John Iacono, 9, John W. McDonough, 5, 24, 27 (bottom), Manny Millan, 7 (bottom), Peter Read Miller, 8, 23, Simon Bruty, 6, 7 (top), Walter Iooss Jr., 25

Design Elements: Shutterstock

Printed in the United States of America.
010054S17

TABLE OF CONTENTS

THE TD LEADER

San Francisco 49ers quarterback Steve Young lofted a pass deep over the middle, aiming for a familiar target. Receiver Jerry Rice adjusted his stride, leaped, outstretched a Raiders defender, snatched the ball out of midair, and tumbled into the end zone. It was his third touchdown of the game. More significantly, it was the 127th of his career, breaking the all-time record for touchdowns by a National Football League (NFL) player.

At the end of the 1993 season, Rice had been just two touchdowns behind Jim Brown on the all-time TD list. Rice surpassed the legendary Browns running back in the first game in the fall of 1994. He torched the Raiders' defense for three touchdowns, including two touchdown catches and one run, which came on a reverse.

Jerry Rice

Before his career was over, Rice scored a total of 208 touchdowns and set dozens of NFL records. Many of those records still stand, and many experts consider Rice the best wide receiver ever to play the game. That's why they call him the G.O.A.T., the Greatest of All Time.

RECORD BREAKERS

RICE'S RECORDS MAY ENDURE NEXT TO STANDARDS SET BY OTHER NFL GREATS. BUT RECORDS ARE MEANT TO BE BROKEN. FOOTBALL FANS LOVE TO SWAP STORIES ABOUT NFL STARS OF THE PAST, AND THEY LOVE TO ROOT FOR TODAY'S PLAYERS AS THEY TRY TO ADD THEIR NAMES TO PRO FOOTBALL'S RECORD BOOK.

LaDainian Tomlinson

MOST CAREER TOUCHDOWNS

1. Jerry Rice (49ers, Raiders, Seahawks), 1985–2004	**208**
2. Emmitt Smith (Cowboys, Cardinals), 1990–2004	**175**
3. LaDainian Tomlinson (Chargers, Jets), 2001–2011	**162**
4. Randy Moss (Vikings, Raiders, Patriots, Titans, 49ers), 1998–2012	**157**
5. Terrell Owens (49ers, Eagles, Cowboys, Bills, Bengals), 1996–2010	**156**

WHAM BAM CAM

The NFL has never witnessed a quarterback like Cam Newton. There have been bigger quarterbacks. There have been faster quarterbacks. And there have been quarterbacks with stronger arms. But no quarterback has ever combined all three skills like Newton does. He poses a serious threat on the ground and through the air.

In a game late in the 2015 season, Newton dove through the line for the 43rd rushing touchdown of his career. The score tied Steve Young's all-time record for rushing touchdowns by a quarterback. Newton reached the mark in just 78 games. It took Young 169 games.

Newton led the Carolina Panthers all the way to Super Bowl 50, played at the conclusion of the 2015 season. He performed brilliantly that season, through the air and on the ground. Newton was named the league's Most Valuable Player (MVP) after throwing 35 touchdown passes and running for 10 scores. His Panthers put up a good fight in the Super Bowl but fell to the Denver Broncos.

Cam Newton

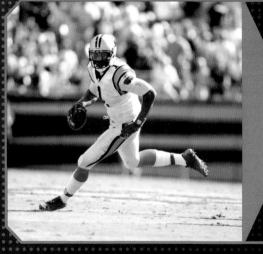

A STRONG START

Cam Newton's incredible talent was immediately apparent. He is the only quarterback to throw for more than 400 yards in his first NFL game. He broke the record for most rushing touchdowns in a single season by a quarterback with 14 in his rookie year.

MOST CAREER RUSHING TOUCHDOWNS, QUARTERBACKS

1. **Cam Newton** (Panthers)	43*
2. **Steve Young** (Buccaneers, 49ers)	43
3. **Kordell Stewart** (Steelers, Bears, Ravens)	38
4. **Steve McNair** (Oilers/Titans, Ravens)	37
5. **Michael Vick** (Falcons, Eagles, Jets, Steelers)	36

*active player; stats through the 2015 season

PRIOR TO HIS NFL CAREER, STEVE YOUNG PLAYED TWO SEASONS FOR THE L.A. EXPRESS IN THE UNITED STATES FOOTBALL LEAGUE, A FAILED RIVAL TO THE NFL. YOUNG RAN FOR NINE TD'S WITH THE EXPRESS. THOSE SCORES DO NOT COUNT IN THE NFL RECORD BOOK.

Steve Young

The St. Louis Rams and Tennessee Titans were deadlocked late in the fourth quarter of Super Bowl XXXIV, which followed the 1999 season. The Rams had been the heavy favorite coming into the game. Their offense, nicknamed "The Greatest Show on Turf," had seemed nearly unstoppable. But the Titans were proving a tough foe. They had just kicked a field goal to tie the score at 16.

The Rams struck quickly on the next drive. Quarterback Kurt Warner dropped back and threw a back-shoulder pass to Isaac Bruce along the right sideline. Bruce caught the ball and dashed through the Titans secondary for the go-ahead touchdown. The 73-yard touchdown pass gave Warner a total of 414 passing yards, the most of any Super Bowl quarterback.

Kurt Warner

When considering the greatest Super Bowl quarterbacks, NFL fans may think of Tom Brady, Joe Montana, Terry Bradshaw, and Troy Aikman. However, it is Kurt Warner who owns the top three positions in the record book for Super Bowl passing yardage. He played in three championship games and threw for more than 350 yards in each one.

However, Warner was on the losing end of two Super Bowls. These losses were both heartbreakers. The New England Patriots defeated his Rams on a last-second field goal in Super Bowl XXXVI. In Super Bowl XLIII, the Pittsburgh Steelers scored on a jaw-dropping last-minute touchdown pass to defeat Warner's Arizona Cardinals.

PASSING YARDS IN A SUPER BOWL

1. **Kurt Warner, Rams** (SB XXXIV)	414
2. **Kurt Warner, Cardinals** (SB XLIII)	377
3. **Kurt Warner, Rams** (SB XXXVI)	365
4. **Donovan McNabb, Eagles** (SB XXXIX)	357
4. **Joe Montana, 49ers** (SB XXIII)	357

ONE-GAME WONDER

Washington's Timmy Smith ran for a record 204 yards in Super Bowl XXII. Smith proved to be a one-hit wonder. During his career, he only managed 602 regular-season yards.

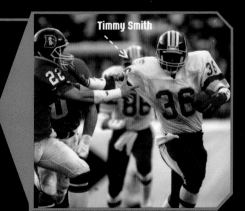

Timmy Smith

On December 9, 1984, Eric Dickerson, running back for the Los Angeles Rams, took a handoff and rumbled nine yards off the right tackle. The run gave Dickerson 2,007 yards, more than any running back had ever gained in a single season. In fact, only one other player, O.J. Simpson, had rushed for more than 2,000 yards in one season. Dickerson added 98 yards in the season's last game for a total of 2,105 yards.

Eric Dickerson

Dickerson had a unique and deceptive running style. Most running backs stay low to the ground when they run. They hunch down to maintain balance as they fend off tacklers. Dickerson ran upright. He took long, elegant strides. He exploded through holes in the line. And when he broke into the open, Dickerson seemed to glide effortlessly down the field.

BARRY SANDERS RETIRED AFTER ONLY 10 SEASONS IN THE NFL, AND MANY EXPERTS THOUGHT HE HAD A GOOD CHANCE TO BECOME THE ALL-TIME RUSHING LEADER. SANDERS AVERAGED 99.8 RUSHING YARDS PER GAME. ALL-TIME LEADER EMMITT SMITH PLAYED 15 SEASONS AND AVERAGED 81.2 RUSHING YARDS PER GAME.

Since Dickerson set the record, five running backs have surpassed the 2,000-yard mark. But Dickerson's record has stood for over 30 years. Vikings superstar Adrian Peterson came close to the mark in 2012. In the last game of the season, he plowed through the Green Bay Packers defense for 199 rushing yards. His gritty 26-yard run set up the Vikings for a last-second game-winning field goal. The win earned his team a trip to the playoffs, but Peterson fell eight yards short of Dickerson's record.

SHORT SEASON, BIG YARDS

In 1973 O.J. Simpson ran for more than 2,000 yards in just 14 games. At the time, that amounted to a full NFL regular season. The other running backs in the 2,000-yard club played 16 games. The NFL expanded the season to 16 games in 1978.

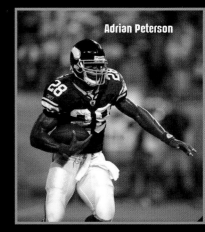

Adrian Peterson

SINGLE-SEASON RUSHING YARDS

1. Eric Dickerson (Rams, 1984)	**2,105**
2. Adrian Peterson (Vikings, 2012)	**2,097**
3. Jamal Lewis (Ravens, 2003)	**2,066**
4. Barry Sanders (Lions, 1997)	**2,053**
5. Terrell Davis (Broncos, 1998)	**2,008**
6. Chris Johnson (Titans, 2009)	**2,006**
7. O.J. Simpson (Bills, 1973)	**2,003**

In 2002 Emmitt Smith broke Walter Payton's record for career rushing yards in typical fashion. Smith followed his fullback into the hole and cut off his right hip for a tough 11-yard gain. It was a solid run. For 15 years, Smith piled solid run on top of solid run until he had gained an astounding 18,355 yards rushing.

Smith was a hard-working running back. He didn't have the breathtaking moves of Payton, the Chicago Bears' legend who broke Jim Brown's record for career rushing yards in 1984. Smith didn't have the brute force of Brown. Smith was durable and dependable. Because he was as solid as a bowling ball and possessed the balance of a gymnast, he could squeeze the most out of every run.

At Smith's induction into the Pro Football Hall of Fame, Jerry Jones, owner of the Dallas Cowboys, explained what made Smith so special. "He always showed up and gave you everything he had," said Jones.

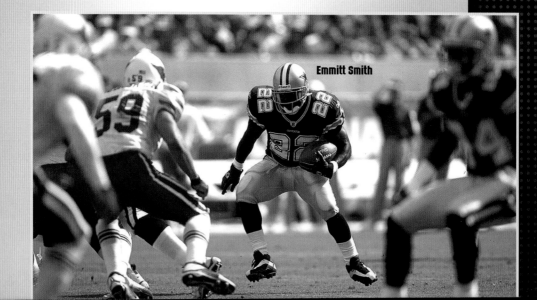

Emmitt Smith

CAREER RUSHING LEADERS

1.	**Emmitt Smith** (Cowboys, Cardinals), 1990–2004	**18,355**
2.	**Walter Payton** (Bears), 1975–1987	**16,776**
3.	**Barry Sanders** (Lions), 1989–1998	**15,269**
4.	**Curtis Martin** (Patriots, Jets), 1995–2005	**14,101**
5.	**LaDainian Tomlinson** (Chargers, Jets), 2001–2011	**13,684**
6.	**Jerome Bettis** (Rams, Steelers), 1993–2005	**13,662**
7.	**Eric Dickerson** (Rams, Colts, Raiders, Falcons), 1983–1993	**13,259**
8.	**Tony Dorsett** (Cowboys, Broncos), 1977–1988	**12,739**
9.	**Jim Brown** (Browns), 1957–1965	**12,312**
10.	**Marshall Faulk** (Colts, Rams), 1994–2005	**12,279**

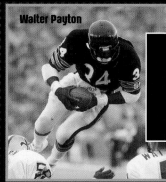

Walter Payton

WALTER PAYTON DIED AT AGE 45 DUE TO A RARE LIVER DISEASE. THE TWO-TIME MVP REMAINS A BELOVED FAVORITE OF BEARS FANS AND FOOTBALL FANS EVERYWHERE.

It couldn't have looked grimmer for the Buffalo Bills at halftime. The Houston Oilers' Run and Shoot offense shredded the Bills defense in the first half of their AFC playoff game in January 1993. The Bills starting quarterback, Jim Kelly, and starting running back, Thurman Thomas, were injured and unable to play. And the Bills offense had trouble moving the ball without them.

But it got even worse. On the Bills' first drive of the second half, the Oilers returned an interception 58 yards for a touchdown. The Bills were trailing 35-3. Swarms of Bills fans headed for the parking lot.

On their second drive, the Bills finally punched the ball into the end zone. On the following kickoff, Bills kicker Steve Christie miraculously recovered his own onside kick. Four plays later, backup quarterback Frank Reich threw a 38-yard touchdown pass. Then the Oilers fell apart. They shanked two punts. They fumbled the snap on a field goal attempt. And they turned the ball over. The Bills offense took advantage of every Oiler misstep. On the strength of four Reich touchdown passes, the Bills scored 35 unanswered points in the second half. The Bills sealed the victory in overtime on a 32-yard field goal.

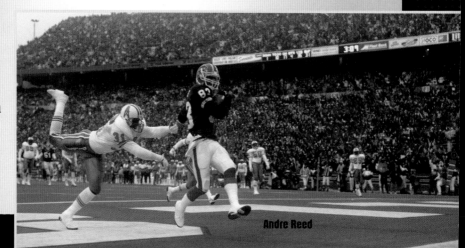

Andre Reed

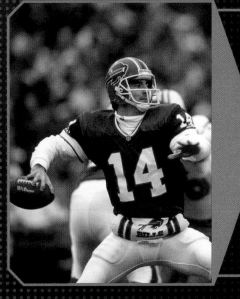

MAGIC FRANK

Frank Reich had a knack for the dramatic. The Miami Hurricanes were pummeling the Maryland Terrapins 31-0 at halftime of the 1984 Orange Bowl. Maryland's coach pulled his starting quarterback in favor of Reich, the backup. Reich threw six touchdown passes in the second half, and Maryland pulled off a miraculous 42-40 victory.

THE NFL'S BIGGEST COMEBACKS

DEFICIT	WINNER	LOSER	DATE
32	Bills	Oilers	Jan. 3, 1993
28	Colts	Chiefs	Jan. 4, 2014
28	49ers	Saints	Dec. 7, 1980
26	Bills	Colts	Sept. 21, 1997
25	Cardinals	Buccaneers	Nov. 8, 1987
25	Browns	Titans	Oct. 5, 2014

FRANK REICH WAS SELECTED BY THE CAROLINA PANTHERS IN THE 1995 EXPANSION DRAFT. HE THREW THE FIRST TOUCHDOWN PASS IN FRANCHISE HISTORY AND STARTED THE FIRST THREE GAMES THE PANTHERS PLAYED.

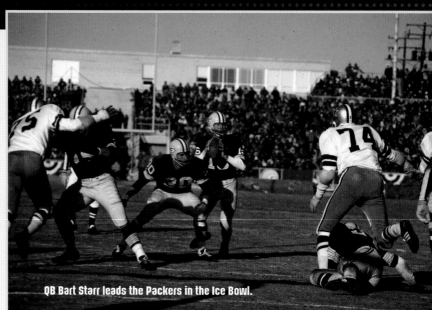

QB Bart Starr leads the Packers in the Ice Bowl.

On December 31, 1967, the air temperature above the frozen tundra of Lambeau Field dropped to 13 degrees below zero Fahrenheit. And on that day, the Green Bay Packers took the field against the Dallas Cowboys for the NFL Championship Game. Nicknamed the "Ice Bowl," it stands as the coldest NFL game ever played. It was also one of the greatest games ever played.

The weather presented problems the players and officials hadn't imagined. After the first play, the referee's extremely cold metal whistle stuck to his lips. He ripped the whistle from his lips, and when they started to bleed, the blood froze. The officials pocketed the whistles and shouted "Stop!" to call the plays dead.

The turf had hardened to the point that the players had trouble staying on their feet. Still, the Packers stormed down the field for two early touchdowns. After that, the Cowboys' "Doomsday" defense squashed the Packers. The Cowboys scored 10 points as a result of two fumble recoveries. In the fourth quarter, Dallas took a 17-14 lead on a 50-yard touchdown pass.

With 4:50 left in the game, however, the Packers' offense started a historic 68-yard march down the field. Quarterback Bart Starr and fullback Chuck Mercein led the Packers down to the 1-yard line. With 16 seconds remaining, Starr dove into the end zone for the victory.

THE FREEZER BOWL

The 1981 AFC Championship Game in Cincinnati's Riverfront Stadium was the NFL's coldest game when considering the windchill factor. The air temperature was minus-9 degrees. Winds reached 27 miles per hour. That meant a windchill factor of minus-59 degrees. The Bengals fought through the polar cold to defeat the Chargers 27-7.

FOOTBALL EXTREMES

DATE	LOCATION	TEAMS	TEMP (F)	WINDCHILL
Dec. 31, 1967	Green Bay	Cowboys at Packers	-13	-48
Jan. 10, 1982	Cincinnati	Chargers at Bengals	-9	-59
Jan. 7, 1996	Kansas City	Colts at Chiefs	-6	-15
Jan. 10, 2016	Minneapolis	Seahawks at Vikings	-6	-25
Jan. 4, 1981	Cleveland	Raiders at Browns	-5	-20
DATE	LOCATION	TEAMS	TEMP (F)	
Sept. 3, 2000	Dallas	Eagles at Cowboys	109.0	
Sept. 30, 2001	Phoenix	Falcons at Cardinals	104.0	
Sept. 23, 2001	Phoenix	Broncos at Cardinals	103.0	
Sept. 21, 2003	Phoenix	Packers at Cardinals	102.0	
Sept. 22, 2002	Phoenix	Chargers at Cardinals	100.0	

Larry Csonka

The 1972 Miami Dolphins exhibited all the traits of an unselfish team. The team would eventually boast six Hall-of-Fame players. During the 1972 season, however, no Dolphin player outshined the team. The Miami defense failed to strike fear in their opponents. Still, it strangled opposing offenses every Sunday. They wore their nickname, the "No-Name Defense," with pride.

While the offense got more attention, no one player emerged as a superstar. Running backs Larry Csonka and Mercury Morris shared the carries. They became the first duo to rush for more the 1,000 yards each in a season. When starting quarterback Bob Griese broke his ankle in Week 5, the Dolphins turned to 38-year-old Earl Morrall. The veteran backup was just four years younger than head coach Don Shula. Still, Morrall kept the team rolling.

The Dolphins struggled against the Pittsburgh Steelers in the AFC Championship game. Tied 7-7 at halftime, Shula replaced Morrall with a healthy Griese. This time Griese turned the game around. He led the Dolphins on two touchdown drives to secure a 21-17 victory. Griese started Super Bowl VII two weeks later. The Dolphins took home the championship and completed the NFL's only perfect season.

BEST NFL SEASON RECORDS
(REGULAR SEASON AND POSTSEASON)

Year	Team	Record
1972	DOLPHINS	17-0
1984	49ERS	18-1
1985	BEARS	18-1
2007	PATRIOTS	18-1
1976	RAIDERS	16-1
1962	PACKERS	14-1

WOE TO THE WINLESS

Year	Team	Record
1960	COWBOYS	0-11-1
1976	BUCCANEERS	0-14
1982	COLTS	0-8-1*
2008	LIONS	0-16

* strike-shortened season

ALMOST PERFECT

The 2007 New England Patriots are the only team to finish a regular NFL season of 16 games undefeated. Tom Brady and the Pats steamrolled opponents all the way to Super Bowl XLII. However, they couldn't finish off the New York Giants. The underdog Giants shocked the football world with a 17-14 victory.

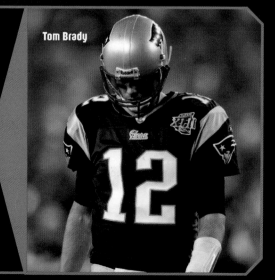

Tom Brady

Brett Favre

On December 5, 2010, a Buffalo Bills linebacker tackled Minnesota Vikings quarterback Brett Favre and drove Favre's throwing shoulder into the turf. The aging QB left the game with numbness through his shoulder and into his hand. He was unable to start the Vikings' following game. It marked the end of Favre's remarkable streak of 297 consecutive starts.

The streak began September 27, 1992, when Favre led the Green Bay Packers to a 17-3 win over the Pittsburgh Steelers. For the next 19 years, Favre took the field. He played despite a separated shoulder, a sprained knee, a broken thumb, a broken foot, and numerous other injuries.

Favre finally left the sport after 20 seasons. He had won a Super Bowl and claimed three MVP trophies, and he retired holding several NFL records.

MOST CONSECUTIVE GAMES PLAYED

PLAYER	POSITION	TOTAL
1. Brett Favre (Packers, Jets, Vikings)	QB	297
2. Jim Marshall (Vikings)	DE	270
3. Mick Tingelhoff (Vikings)	C	240
4. Bruce Matthews (Oilers/Titans)	OL	229
5. Will Shields (Chiefs)	RG	223

Favre's former backup in Green Bay, Matt Hasselbeck, once said of the streak, "It's beyond reason. It's ridiculous. He's gotten lucky a little bit, too. But he's just the toughest guy in the world." Many football experts believe Favre's consecutive starts record is unbreakable. The closest active player is more than 100 games behind Favre's mark.

UNBREAKABLE RECORDS?

Many fans consider these records to be unbreakable. What do you think?

14 interceptions in a season	Dick Lane, Rams
7.0 sacks in a game	Derrick Thomas, Chiefs
40 points in a game	Ernie Nevers, Cardinals
81 career interceptions	Paul Krause, Vikings
347 coaching victories	Don Shula, Colts/Dolphins

DEMPSEY'S MIGHTY BOOT

The Detroit Lions kicked a field goal to take a 17-16 lead with 11 seconds left in a 1970 game. On the ensuing kickoff, the New Orleans Saints returned the ball to their 30-yard line. After a quick 17-yard completion, the Saints called a timeout. One of the Saints coaches yelled, "Tell Stumpy to get ready."

Stumpy was the nickname of the Saints placekicker Tom Dempsey. Dempsey ran onto the field for what seemed to be a hopeless field goal attempt. But his mighty kick cleared the crossbar. The 63-yard field goal gave the Saints a win.

Dempsey had been born without four fingers on his right hand and without toes on his right foot. He wore a special shoe, custom-built for kicking. After the record-breaking field goal, Tex Schramm, president of the Dallas Cowboys, protested the use of Dempsey's kicking shoe. But the NFL had already approved the shoe. It was lighter than the regulation shoe and had a flat front.

Tom Dempsey

Dempsey's 63-yard field goal shattered the previous record by seven yards. It would be 28 years until Jason Elam equaled it and 43 years until Matt Prater kicked a 64-yard field goal.

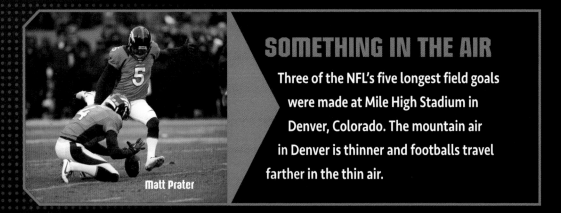

SOMETHING IN THE AIR

Three of the NFL's five longest field goals were made at Mile High Stadium in Denver, Colorado. The mountain air in Denver is thinner and footballs travel farther in the thin air.

Matt Prater

RECORD-SETTING KICKS

YARDS	KICKER	GAME	DATE
64	MATT PRATER	BRONCOS VS. TITANS	DEC. 8, 2013
63	TOM DEMPSEY	SAINTS VS. LIONS	NOV. 8, 1970
63	JASON ELAM	BRONCOS VS. JAGUARS	OCT. 25, 1998
63	SEBASTIAN JANIKOWSKI	RAIDERS AT BRONCOS	SEPT. 12, 2011
63	DAVID AKERS	49ERS AT PACKERS	SEPT. 9, 2012

DEMPSEY'S HEROICS INSPIRED LOUISIANA NATIVE BOBBY BRIDGER TO WRITE A SONG CALLED "THE MIGHTY BOOT OF DEMPSEY."

PEYTON'S SWAN SONG

November 15, 2015, was a bittersweet day for Peyton Manning. The sweet part arrived in the first quarter of the Denver Broncos game against the Kansas City Chiefs. Manning hit Ronnie Hillman in the flat for a 4-yard gain. The completion put Manning atop Brett Favre for the most passing yards of any quarterback in NFL history. The rest of Manning's day was dreadful. He completed just 5 of 20 pass attempts and threw four interceptions. In the third quarter, Broncos coach Gary Kubiak benched Manning, one of the greatest quarterbacks to ever button up a chinstrap.

Weeks later Manning reclaimed the Broncos' starting quarterback position. In a 23-16 divisional playoff win over the Pittsburgh Steelers, he led a fourth quarter touchdown drive with the game on the line. In the AFC Championship Game, Manning faced his greatest rival, Tom Brady, and Brady's New England Patriots. The 39-year-old met the challenge with two touchdown passes and a crucial 12-yard first down scramble to help Denver to a 20-18 win. In Super Bowl 50, Manning struggled against the Carolina Panthers stout defense, but the Broncos' own impressive defense carried the team to a 24-10 victory.

Payton Manning

Manning struggled statistically throughout the 2015 season. But despite his injuries, he found ways to win. Manning announced his retirement after the Super Bowl, leaving the game as a champion.

CAREER PASSING YARDS (REGULAR SEASON)

1. **Peyton Manning** (Colts, Broncos), 1998–2015	71,940
2. **Brett Favre** (Packers, Jets, Vikings), 1991–2010	71,838
3. **Dan Marino** (Dolphins), 1983–1999	61,361
4. **Drew Brees** (Chargers, Saints), 2001–	60,903*
5. **Tom Brady** (Patriots), 2000–	58,028*

*active player; stats through 2015

THE MAD SCRAMBLER

Dan Marino passed Fran Tarkenton's 47,003 career passing yards in 1995. Known as "The Mad Scrambler," Tarkenton starred for the Giants and Vikings during his long career. He owned the yardage record for 19 years, longer than any other quarterback.

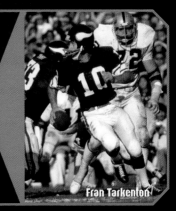
Fran Tarkenton

Deacon Jones

"Sacking the quarterback is like devastating a city." Those were the words of Deacon Jones, the man who coined the term "sack." Jones played on one of the most revered defensive lines in NFL history, the L.A. Rams' "Fearsome Foursome." He reinvented the defensive end position, smacking offensive lineman off balance and using his great quickness to get to the quarterback.

But the official sack records do not list Jones. He played before the NFL started tracking sacks as an official statistic. According to estimates, Jones sacked the quarterback more than 170 times. Other star linemen from his era and earlier years also had their sack stats go unrecognized.

In the 1980s and 1990s, Reggie White rose to the top of the official list. White weighed 300 pounds, yet he was as quick as a cat and as strong as a bear. In his first eight NFL seasons, the "Minister of Defense" sacked the quarterback 124 times in only 121 games. White retired in 2000 with an NFL record of 198 sacks.

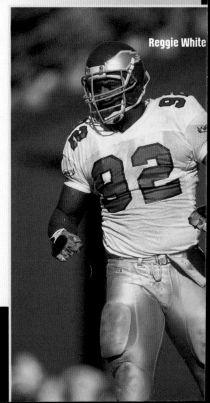

Reggie White

His record didn't stand for long. On December 7, 2003, Washington Redskins lineman Bruce Smith dropped New York Giants quarterback Jesse Palmer for the 199th sack of his career. Smith added another sack that season, ending his career with an even 200. His record has lasted ever since.

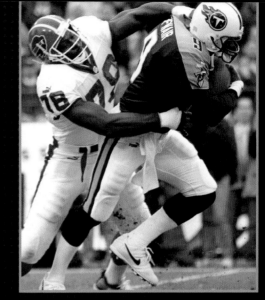

Bruce Smith

CAREER SACK TOTALS

PLAYER	SACKS	YEARS
Bruce Smith (Bills, Redskins)	200.0	1985–2003
Reggie White (Eagles, Packers, Panthers)	198.0	1985–2000
Kevin Greene (Rams, Steelers, Panthers, 49ers)	160.0	1985–1999
Chris Doleman (Vikings, Falcons, 49ers)	150.5	1985–1999
Michael Strahan (Giants)	141.5	1993–2007

CHASING THE RECORD

The chase is on to pass 200 sacks. A crop of talented defensive lineman, including DeMarcus Ware and J.J. Watt, have a genuine chance to reach and exceed 200 sacks. They are the new sack kings. NFL quarterbacks beware!

J.J. Watt

THE LOWLY KICKER?

In 1998 the Minnesota Vikings' Gary Anderson delivered the NFL's first perfect season for a placekicker. Anderson attempted 35 field goals and 59 extra points, and he made all of them. In the 1998 NFC Championship game, with just over two minutes remaining, Anderson missed a 38-yard field goal. The Atlanta Falcons quickly tied the game. Then the Falcons won the game in overtime on a 38-yard field goal by Morten Andersen (no relation to Gary).

Placekickers have been the punch line of a lot of jokes over the years. *Who's the guy that hangs out with the football team?* The kicker. *Who's the little guy with the clean uniform?* The kicker. Kickers don't get much respect. Some people say they don't play *real* football. They don't tackle or block. They only trot onto the field for a handful of plays.

Gary Anderson

But placekickers are among the most valuable players in football. The power and accuracy of their legs lead to heartbreak and celebration every week of each NFL season. Like Morten Andersen, they receive little notice when they are exceptional. Like Gary Anderson, they take all the blame when they miss a crunch-time kick.

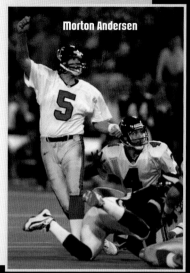

Morton Andersen

Placekickers score more points than any other players in the league. In fact, kickers hold the top 34 spots on the NFL career points scored leader board. Morten Andersen is number one, and Gary Anderson is number two.

NFL POINTS LEADERS

PLAYER	POINTS	YEARS	POSITION
Morten Andersen (Saints, Falcons, Giants, Chiefs, Vikings)	2,544	1982–2007	K
Gary Anderson (Steelers, Eagles, 49ers, Vikings, Titans)	2,434	1982–2004	K
Adam Vinatieri (Patriots, Colts)	2,253	1996–2015	K
Jason Hanson (Lions)	2,150	1992–2012	K
John Carney (Buccaneers, Rams, Chargers, Saints, Jaguars, Chiefs, Giants)	2,062	1988–2010	K

KICKER ADAM VINATIERI WENT UNDRAFTED AFTER COLLEGE BUT BECAME THE ONLY NFL PLAYER TO SCORE 1,000 OR MORE POINTS WITH TWO FRANCHISES. HE HAS ALSO MADE TWO LAST-SECOND KICKS TO WIN SUPER BOWLS.

GLOSSARY

defensive end—lineman who often rushes the quarterback

fullback—running back who is often used as a blocker

linebacker—defensive player who lines up behind the linemen; there are usually three or four linebackers who act as the second line of defense

line of scrimmage—imaginary line across the field determined by the referee's placement of the ball after the previous play

offensive tackle—offensive lineman who blocks defenders on the outside of the line; offensive tackles line up outside of guards, who line up next to the center

onside kick—an attempt by the kicking team to recover the football on the kickoff

post route—a pass route in which a receiver runs straight up the field, then breaks diagonally across the middle of the field toward the goal post

sack—the tackling of the quarterback behind the line of scrimmage as he is attempting to pass

veteran—a player who has a lot of experience playing football

windchill factor—the "feels like" temperature that results from the air temperature and wind speed

READ MORE

Doeden, Matt. *Fantasy Football Math*. North Mankato, Minn.: Capstone Press, 2016.

Frederick, Shane. *Football Stats and the Stories Behind Them: What Every Fan Needs to Know*. North Mankato, Minn.: Capstone Press, 2016.

The Editors of Sports Illustrated Kids. *The Big Book of Who Football*. New York: Sports Illustrated, 2015.

INTERNET SITES

FactHound offers a safe, fun way to find Internet sites related to this book. All of the sites on FactHound have been researched by our staff.

Here's all you do:
Visit *www.facthound.com*

Type in this code: 9781515737612

INDEX